The Long Conversation

The Long Conversation

poems

DAVID DOOLEY

Story Line Press | Pasadena, CA

The Long Conversation
Copyright © 2021 by David Dooley
All Rights Reserved

ISBN 978-1-58654-073-9 (tradepaper)
    978-1-58654-087-6 (casebound)

The National Endowment for the Arts, the Los Angeles County Arts Commission, the Ahmanson Foundation, the Dwight Stuart Youth Fund, the Max Factor Family Foundation, the Pasadena Tournament of Roses Foundation, the Pasadena Arts & Culture Commission and the City of Pasadena Cultural Affairs Division, the City of Los Angeles Department of Cultural Affairs, the Audrey & Sydney Irmas Charitable Foundation, the Kinder Morgan Foundation, the Meta & George Rosenberg Foundation, the Allergan Foundation, the Riordan Foundation, Amazon Literary Partnership, and the Mara W. Breech Foundation partially support Red Hen Press.

First Edition
Published by Story Line Press
an imprint of Red Hen Press
www.redhen.org

Acknowledgments

Some of the poems in this book originally appeared in other publications, including *Beloit Poetry Journal, The Hudson Review, Mississippi Arts & Letters, New Texas '91,* and *The Reaper.* I would especially like to thank the late Frederick Morgan and the other editors of *The Hudson Review* for their loyal belief in my work and for publishing ten of the poems included here.

I would also like to thank all the friends who read drafts of my work in Knoxville, San Antonio, and elsewhere. Special thanks go to the late Allen Hoey for the attention he brought to all of these poems. Special thanks, too, to George Drew for helping me put this volume together; and to Red Hen Press and everyone else who worked to bring these books back into print.

For George

CONTENTS

PREFACE

Rereading *The Volcano Inside* and *The Revenge by Love* thirty years later brings back many memories and emotions, especially memories of friends. Indeed, the hidden theme of *The Volcano Inside* is friendship, for most of the poems are about friends who are usually not identified by name.

There are so many people to be grateful to, especially everyone who read these and many other poems in various drafts; those who chose individual poems for publication; and, of course, Robert McDowell, Lysa McDowell, and Mark Jarman, who selected *The Volcano Inside* as the first winner of the Nicholas Roerich Prize for Story Line Press. Lysa McDowell, who did such a wonderful job designing the cover and choosing the typeface for the book, discovered my manuscript among the three hundred or so entered in the Story Line competition.

A little bit of cultural history: neither of the schools I attended as an undergraduate (Tennessee and Johns Hopkins) offered classes in the writing of poetry. At that time, most universities did not. Though I took numerous courses in poetry, I did not write poetry until several years later. A professor friend kept asking me to critique his haiku, and I gladly did so until one night when I thought, "Well, darn it, I want to make him read my poems for a change," and sat down and wrote ten haiku. This wasn't the most romantic beginning a poet ever had, but it worked.

Like many first books of poetry that eventually get published, *The Volcano Inside* wasn't really a first volume. There were three predecessors, and it was my good fortune that none of those was ever published. Three poems from those early manuscripts did make their way into *Volcano*; "Johnson at 34," the earliest, was probably written in May of 1979. I have never dated poems or drafts, so the chronology is a bit hazy. Except for those three, the other poems in *Volcano* were written after I moved from Knoxville to San Antonio in 1982. My recollection is that from 1982-1984 I wrote few if any poems, but that changed after I attended a writers' conference at Wells College in the summer of 1985. The stimulating environment and the new friendships sparked real growth in my work. As happens with many poets, an increase in technical skill led to poetic subjects of more complexity and depth, and more challenging subjects then led to further technical demands.

Most of the poems in the present collection were written between 1985 and 1987. I believe that most or all of the Georgia O'Keeffe poems in *The Revenge by Love* were written by the time *The Volcano Inside* was chosen for publication by Story Line, and had it not found a publisher, the manuscript for the next round of competitions would have included the O'Keeffe sequence. All of the poems in *The Revenge by Love* were written by 1991, when Story Line Press accepted the manuscript, although the book was not published until 1995.

The late Allen Hoey had a great deal to do with forming the manuscript of *The Volcano Inside*, originally called *Take Five*. I remember talking to Allen one night after I'd given a poetry reading at Ithaca College. At that time he was living in a drafty trailer outside of town. I believe it was September, a high summer month back in Texas, and Allen, a native of upstate New York, was highly amused that I thought it was cold enough that I sat wrapped up in a blanket as we talked. Enthusiastic about some of the newer, longer-lined poems, Allen said, "We've got to get you published." Over the next few weeks each of us made lists of A poems (must include), B poems (might include), and C poems (probably not). We discussed and considered and argued, and the compromise solution was that every poem Allen wanted in went in, and every poem Allen wanted out went out. I came to appreciate that Allen had a better grasp of my work than I did.

For his own first book, *A Fire in the Cold House of Being* (chosen for the Camden Prize by Galway Kinnell), Allen had hit on the strategy of putting the stranger and quirkier poems in the middle section. However, because so many of my poems belonged in the strange and quirky category, both of us instantly realized that we would need instead to play up the difference of the manuscript and should place "How I Wrote It" as the first poem. This turned out to be the right move.

Many of the poems being published by other poets in the 1980s were in the confessional mode, short-lined, with much use of images, similes, and attention-getting line breaks. On the other hand, most of the poems in *The Volcano Inside* and *The Revenge by Love* were about persons other than myself. The word "I" in both books does not usually refer to the author. *The Volcano Inside* has two poems about fathers, neither of them mine. In those days I never felt more like myself than when I was writing about other people.

The poems in both books generally proceed from dramatic or narrative approaches, and often use longer lines with considerable enjambment. In addition to traditional dramatic monologues like "The Reading" and "How I Wrote It," oblique monologues like "First Love," "Revelation," and "A Little Hunger" make use of the limited omniscient point of view, which is unusual in poetry though common in fiction.

It seems natural to me to work with various levels of diction, perhaps because of my background as a Southerner. Southerners who grew up during the twentieth century had access to an unusually vital literary language, with high, middle, and low styles all a part of the common culture. The King James Bible, an important part of civic as well as religious life, provided the high style; the standard English we learned at school and some of us spoke at home provided the middle style; and a Southern dialect rich in vivid expressions and proverbial phrases provided the low style. One of the greatest gifts a writer can receive is a lively non-literary language, with delight in words by those whose language is primarily spoken rather than written.

Art, literature, and music are also important themes of the poems, particularly in *The Revenge by Love*. After I read at the Nicholas Roerich Museum in New York, the director of the museum said to me, "You write orchestrally," a comment which pleased me greatly, for at that time I was listening almost daily to classical music.

Changes from the original are relatively minor. For the most part, I have resisted the temptation to rewrite the poems. A couple of words were changed in one poem, a couple of line breaks in another. Two poems have been dropped from the first section of *The Revenge by Love*, which now seems tighter. The sequence of poems in *The Volcano Inside* has been changed.

The late Donald Hall wrote an appreciative review of *The Volcano Inside*, and we began to correspond. I was able to meet him in the late 1990s when he read in San Diego, where I had moved. He told me I looked like I was supposed to: the exact opposite of my poems. A few days later I sent him a note saying how nice it was to meet him. He responded that after he returned home, he had had a manic episode, and as a result he had almost no recollection of his trip to California. All of which sounds rather like one of my poems.

After the two Story Line books, which I am happy to combine in one volume here, I would go on to explore a variety of forms of prose poems (*The Living Among the Dying*, poems about AIDS, never published; and *The Zen Garden*, out of print); return to a more meditative style; compose a full-length book of poems about the Labors of Hercules; and even write poems where "I" refers to someone not unlike myself. But those are stories for other occasions.

The Long Conversation

PART I

The Volcano Inside

(1988)

THE READING

You see auras, do you not? No? You will,
and very soon. I could tell when you came in,
you were using your psychic, trying to figure out
what this old gal was up to. And that's good!
Just settle back in that armchair, put your feet up,
the gizmo is there on the side, honey, and I'll sit down here
in my special chair. As many times as I've sat here to give a reading,
this chair must be more psychic than most so-called fortune tellers.
Close your eyes if it helps. Your aura is lovely,
I see the purple and the silver-white and the healing green,
but there is a lime green you need to get rid of.
You are truly, in the deepest sense, a beautiful soul.
You have a highly spiritual nature, you want to
float on the mystery of life like a boat on a still lagoon.
For you the mind, and you have a good mind, is not enough,
you want to press beyond the veils. Now I know
there'll be questions you want to ask, but just hang on,
I may give you the answer before you ask the question!
That big one, the question you're dying to ask,
the answer is no. I don't hold out any hope.
Now when I say you have a spiritual nature,
and I truly believe you may have a mission
as one of the forerunners of the New Age, I don't mean to suggest
you don't care what's going on on this planet,
because you most definitely do, and furthermore, you are a,
how shall I say this, a very healthy woman. And your husband,
you're not wearing a ring, it's in your purse tied up in a handkerchief,

well, your all's romantic fires don't burn as brightly
as they once did. And this other man you wanted to ask me about,
oh, a beautiful soul, I can't see his eyes or hair,
kind of skinny like, a beautiful, magnanimous soul,
but nothing but trouble for you. He's not a redhead.
There's already been one redheaded man in your life,
and that was enough. My first husband was redheaded,
and one day he up and de-camped with a blonde but brown at the roots
divorcee from down the street, and me with six kids.
This man you're so crazy about, he won't ever leave his wife.
Now I'm not one to speak out against romance, but you can't
live in fairyland all your life, so wake up, Cinderella,
and get out of that pumpkin! Your children—
three of them, isn't it—that youngest one's a real scamp,
I can see that grin of his. He leads a charmed life,
the girls are going to be all over him. Just remember
to be firm with him, he needs it, and the oldest boy,
different as day and night. You shouldn't worry about him,
he's serious and takes things hard, but he'll come through.
Solid. Rock solid. He won't tell you how much you mean to him,
but you'll know. That daughter of yours, what can we say about her?
She's just like you, only even more stubborn, she's a rebel
the way you never were. I can see her as a little girl,
stomping that foot up and down, "I won't do it!
I won't do it!"—doesn't matter what.
Let me soothe your mind about one thing, I don't see
anything bad happening to her. Oh, sorrow and unhappiness,
yes Lord, plenty of that, but nothing bad. She's got a nose
that can smell out any man that's wrong for her

no matter where he's hiding. Let her go her own way,
since she will regardless, love her when you can,
and if she starts throwing things, don't forget to duck!
Your husband's a good man, you have to provoke him
to get mad, just so you can get mad at him,
I can see you off in the corner sulking up a storm.
The two of you are not soulmates, your soulmate
did not take earthly shape during this incarnation,
but wait till the lifetime after next! My new husband
and I are soulmates, but why did he wait to show up
till I was fat and fifty? Everything happens for a purpose,
that's what I've always known in my bones, and that's what
my guides tell me. Your husband will never understand you,
but he loves you. You're the only poetry he's ever known.
What lies ahead for you two isn't clear to me, though I don't see
any major changes in your life anytime soon. I'm sorry,
I know that's not the answer you wanted. One thing I do see
is your interest in the spiritual becoming greater and greater,
and if you feel the need to meet with like-minded souls,
the study group meets right here every Thursday at seven.
Whew! I don't see another thing. Every time after one of these
I feel like I've been rode hard and put away wet.
There's coffee on the stove, and this cigarette, if I can light it,
is going to taste mighty good. And remember this, dear,
the ones in the shining robes never fail to provide light.
Have a cinnamon roll with your coffee—homemade.
I feel the need for a taste of sweet when I come back down.

THE WOMAN ON THE BEACH

Blown along like the sand, she walks, alone for once,
on the beach, not venturing into the scrub,
for sometimes, back in the dunes,
a smell like sour watermelon rinds
warns of a rattler. A beach ball, swirled in
blue and yellow and red, hops toward her,
and she smiles, picks it up and bounces it
toward a happy squealer, younger version of her own,
those five nearest her, products of bloody parturition.
And seated there, admonishing in a cheerful
practiced voice, is one of her own kind,
a sacrificer. Selves are expendable:
they build cabins in the woods, tremble at a touch,
seek gurus in Tibet, open boutiques.
But the one faith, Yggdrasil, Valhalla-upholding,
grows in place concentrically, choking all smaller greens.
The gulls flap above the waves like flying baby bottles.
Foam glides over her feet. Time to turn back,
though for a few minutes longer she can stroll,
unencumbered by solicitude. The portion of Martha is bitter:
to bake the bread and be rebuked for it.
Like the fabled bird, she would rip her breast open
should her young require. In the shallows
mother and child are digging with tiny shovels.
Sandpipers run to their prey on cartoon tiptoes.
In the distance, near the horizon, gray pelicans ride the waves.

THE LOVERS

He read the baseball scores out loud across the cereal bowls
because she didn't care, liquidly telling of Blue Jays and Tigers,
the half-smile that wanted a woman's attention.
True that she had him for a few days only,
that was all she needed, lacking eternity.
She memorized the lines he wrote for her:

> *How the dark lake clung to the white forms,*
> *and they flipped over on their backs,*
> *above them the star-thickets,*
> *like music shocked to visibility.*

So like him, not to include in his verse how after
they toweled each other in the chilling air
and made love near a clump of eel grass,
he grabbed her wool skirt and threatened to toss it in the water.
It was provoking, when she offered him more coffee
and passed the cream pitcher—real cream, not milk—
that he had no idea what she was willing to do,
how lightly she would fling them aside, husband, children, honor,
should he say the word—oh, he said so many words,
and wrote, too, but not the only words the thought of which
had power to bring her here. No doubt he thought her
incapable of irony, as she stirred thick cream in her Cajun coffee
and bit into the loaf spread thick with raspberry jam.
He flapped open his terrycloth robe and belched
to test her sensibilities, the bad little boy smile
firmly in place. Just like a man, not seeking
the forgiveness he didn't expect he needed.
That would be her consolation back in the other world,

that he would never know how she forgave him
for leaving her life as it was.
She declined his offer of help with the dishes—
wouldn't he be full of himself if he washed them—dunked the plates
into the soapy water, while he whistled and, she could tell,
caressed in imagination each fold of her body—so when
she swung around, snapped, "I've got a better idea.
Let your damn wife do the dishes!" and ran out the door,
not even grabbing a towel for her slippery hands,
he didn't, not just for a moment, start to run after her.

TARKLIN VALLEY

"I lived in a bygone age," he says,
"and I'm twenty-eight.
My father would ford the stream here
in his '46 Chevy. You can't any more,
the cars are too low."
He jabs at the water with a stick.
"Look at the beetles motorboating around."

Where he used to swim.
Boys perch on the railing.
Are they sixteen, seventeen?
"Farm boys peak early,
then it's downhill."

Clouds hang
in the even heat.
He backs up the car to show me a passionflower.
I can't see him in these fenced-off fields.
I think about friendship,
easy, impotent.
We walk and rest in it.

Eusebia Church, with the graves in front of it.
"My family is buried in rows here.
Look how neat they are."
I turn my back to the road and piss in the churchyard.
"I need to get back to the city," he says.
We drive slowly off.
"There's love here, but that's not enough." I agree.

LAST DAYS

That was all she could manage today,
a few bites of the chicken, cut up small, and some
of the applesauce. A few sips of milk.
Always that way when the other women died.
This was the third. How could she know, too deaf
to hear the months of hymn-singing, vision
too dim for more than shapes moving closer,
shapes moving farther away. Perhaps she sensed it
like an amoeba, withdrawing from anything
that touched. She knew him sometimes, sometimes
she said words. He was becoming like a nurse,
matter-of-fact about death, commiserating gently
before or after the moment, but with tasks of his own
to think of. Harder now, walking there every day,
heart beating fast till he'd have to stop for breath.
Mrs. Kitts drove him home after her shift, kind of her,
he'd asked her in for coffee a few times. No liquor,
her church saw to that. "Do you like living alone?"
she asked him once, fiddling with her beehive,
in a voice that let him know she knew some people did.
All he said was he didn't mind. It was hard to explain
that it didn't matter any more, happiness. If only
he'd known that years ago. Others had been happy,
and what had it gotten them? There were nights,
bourbon low in the bottle, when he could wish for a companion,
they would listen to Bach follow God in the endless fugues.
If the heart got him, what would happen to her?
Not that they weren't good, they wouldn't let her lie in her own filth,
but who would take the time? Once he crouched under the japonica,
he must have been six, sobbing for the Lord to sweep him away

up into heaven. He was never one of her favorites.
Tomorrow was Friday: fish sticks and probably potatoes.
On the walk, when he'd have to catch his breath,
he'd stop by the vacant lot, where primroses
grew as thick as mushrooms. In a few days
she'd be right back to where she was before.

SONG WITHOUT WORDS

We set out looking for eagles.
Gulls hovered near the boat
and terns bobbed for fish in the green water.
When we sailed into the river,
we were able to go with the wind.
An ancient oak on the rock face
twisted its roots to the lake,
roots longer than the tree was tall.
A double-breasted cormorant,
all black so it had to be female,
dived, rose up with a fish in her beak,
then skimmed the water to a piece of driftwood
where she perched,
letting the wind dry her heavy wings.
The limestone hills were covered with prickly pear
and with Spanish dagger,
the creamy blooms like a giant hyacinth.
Then the falls: four streams from one broad channel
poured into the river.
On the clifftop a black Spanish goat
gave suck to her kid, when all at once
he butted against her and over she fell.
Nanny and kid cried out,
her hooves struck the rocks.
On the fourth try she scrambled to her feet,
then sank again to her knees, surprisingly calm.
She looked as if she would wait, and try again,

and nibble the nearby grass,
till at last she could leap up the rocks.
As we sailed upriver, a pair of hawks,
redtails by the look of them,
circled around each other slowly.
We looked for a nest high up in the hills.
Below Buzzard's Roost, at the huge outcropping of limestone
shaped like a mushroom, we looked for a waterfall,
a torrent just after a heavy rain.
Today, a trickle.
We saw movement rather than water,
a downward force the sunlight turned into crystals
and flung to the rocks below.
Where were the eagles? We were too late.
They had flown back to their nests,
northward and westward,
to Colorado, Wyoming, the coast of Alaska.
But the turkey vultures V'd over the river
and flapped their wings a little, and soared a little,
and hung in the March air over the cliffs.
The waves crumpled before our approach.
We counted eight snapping turtles
sunning themselves on a rotten log.
How far had we gone? Lampasas County?
Time to maneuver the boat around
if we wanted to get back before dusk.
Through the dense brush on the western bank

white-tailed deer were cropping the stubble.
Heading into the wind, and the wind stronger,
both of us tired as the horizon goldened.
Back in a cove we noticed a bird flying,
not especially high, its wings held even.
Wings held perfectly level, as the eagle flies.
A bald eagle. Male, still immature,
the breast beginning to feather white.
Next year he would mate for life;
both would return to winter in these gray hills.
We said nothing while the wind ruffled our jackets.
The eagle dipped and ascended, sank and rose into view.

JOHNSON AT 34

Life will be great
now that I've outlived Jesus.
Today at school I should have opened the door,
flung out my arms and said,
"It's my birthday, I get to fuck any woman I want."
Ten years ago today was one of the five best days
of my life. I climbed a firetower in the Ozarks
with Allen Ginsberg. We saw everything,
I'll never forget it.
Irish whiskey for dessert?
It's my birthday, boy, and I love the taste.
What do I want? I want to be great, fucked,
famous, and loved, in that order.

MORNING RUN

Lace up the Nikes and take off out of there,
run away from the house as if it were on fire
just because you are. Don't bother to warm up
or jog easily past the first two houses, habits can be broken
out of necessity, you keep telling yourself that,
and what's a muscle strain? Pound deep
into the pavement, for it wrecks the knees.
Clench the arms high and strangle the air from your fists.
Turn the corner and the damnable house is gone, save for a glimpse
across the alley trashcans. Start the climb of the hill
so shoes squish in the dawn grass and lungs gasp
at the steepness. Swear out loud and charge over the top
onto the high-school track. Hear the cinders crunch
as you run the first lap. One, one and a half, two,
throw everything into that circular path, run, run,
chest on fire. All that you wanted years ago
squats on the living room rug. Sweat out the words "I want"
till the ooze glisters and drops to the ground.
Breathe, contract, three and a half, four,
nothing alive but the breath. Yes, at last, now,
fly while you have the chance, fly, the finger of the god
has touched you. Let this gilded humanstuff
gather itself and it shall transform all. Round and round
and the air brightens. Count the laps: eight? no, nine,
and down the hill, dawnrunner, touch the earth lightly,
this was created for you. See how the shingled houses
hold skyward their second stories. Think of the lives lived there.
Slacken the pace on the back block. Angle across and approach

by the other direction. Slow to a trot for the last few meters.
Turn the knob gently and ease up the back stairs.
Peel off the drenched shorts and top and set the water steaming.
Scrub, scrub, all is erased from your body. Stand by the cloudy glass,
numb and naked. Wrap yourself in the satin robe
and listen for sounds that the others may be awaiting you.
Go downstairs for what could be a day of a kind of happiness.

FIRST LOVE

Late. He was late. Lately he was late,
and later on he'd still be late. Oops, the home-grown
was getting her a little high after all. The photograph,
the way the sun was shining on the wedding picture
on the TV. Neat. It was sweet how he'd drug out that picture
the morning after she came back. He hadn't thrown it away.
She'd hidden one picture, just one picture of him,
where Doyle would never think to look. As if she'd known.
But what business was it of Doyle's, Ricky was part of her life,
you couldn't pretend like part of your life never happened,
the father of your child, that had to count for something.
What time was it anyway? She could watch TV,
it was fun to watch the soaps stoned. *Another World*
was getting good, they'd brought back Cecile,
she was married to a king or something and she'd kidnapped Cass,
so Kathleen, who was out of her wheelchair, didn't know whether
to cry for being jilted or search to the ends of the earth
for the man she loved. Later than she'd thought: cartoons.
Grass could do that, remember the time Ricky spent all afternoon
staring at a Pink Floyd album cover. Freaked him out
when he saw it was dark outside. You had to be stoned
or else a little kid to like cartoons, they didn't make much sense.
Unless you could see it as kind of symbolical,
bashing each other on the head, like good guys and bad guys.
Brandon could watch them by the hour. Like when she came back
after Granny's funeral, and Brandon wasn't crying any more,
just sitting on the couch next to Doyle watching cartoons.

Doyle was really a better lover than Ricky, but folks were right,
you shouldn't confuse sex with love. It was funny,
back in the tenth grade Ricky wasn't even that interested
when she'd happen to be standing near his locker,
and now they were in each other's blood. The lies some people told,
he wasn't selling the stuff, he simply knew where to buy.
God, it would be good right now, you could smoke it like pot
and suddenly you were happy. If he was your man,
right and wrong just didn't enter into it at all.
Maybe the Catholics were right, you could only marry once,
divorce and getting married again meant nothing to the Lord.
You know, the idea of a man turning into a spider
and climbing up buildings was dumb and sort of repulsive
if you stopped to think about it. But Brandon loved that show.
Where in the world was Ricky? She might as well
lie down and take a nap. That would be nice,
to go to sleep and wake up with Ricky standing over her.

LETTING IT DIE

Letting it die: not killing it,
that would be a mistake; the Doberman unleashed
by an innocent syllable, and padding bloody-mouthed
to cringe at the master's footstool; but letting it die—
not forcing the drowning man under, nailmarks
on your neck, but idling on the sand in the twilight,
the wind teasing away the bobbings and the cry. No,
you do not understand, my little sister, in your heavy
brocaded peasant dress, as we drink Kenyan coffee
on a late Saturday morning. Even before I say, "I met
someone yesterday," you're ready from the hesitation
and the unwilling smile to say, "I'm so glad." All right: we glanced,
our eyes barometers; play of intelligence over a dark face;
disengagements interspersed as the worldly ones do. We met by
casualness, proving our experience; parleyed in bright
sophistications; he half-turned toward me, matching
my stance, before he withdrew; mine for the patience.
You know, little sister, the underneath as well as I:
consubstantiation of fears, old dreams of doubleness, and
frenzied adoration. Once, what joy; such meeting's agar-agar
for a phantasmagoria of riches. This is the bliss
that poisons daily happiness. Any morning will do:
drive in the dark to the airport, a red-clad stewardess
offers juice, four tulip trees on the boulevard with their
fat mauve blossoms—magic unless his image leaches through.
Unfaithful? surely; my adamant his millstone; cold lash of
wit destroying silence. Letting it die: no faith in it.
Able to touch the shoulders under his robe, though

a touch may push away. The rush of blood sickens
like the onset of flu. Never to you, little sister?
Letting it die. More coffee, yes. (Side by side we stood,
rapt in the silvery spell of the coloratura.)

FATHER

Yes, they were going home. Summer afternoon. Stop first, though,
for a beer at Piggy's Grill. "You wait here." Rolled down the windows.
They knew enough not to get out of the car, Mama too.
Going to get drunk. Nobody said it, not even Junior.
"Get your hands off me." "Children, be good." "I hate him."
How does she sit there. Hard on the little ones. "It's hot."
"Oh look, here he comes now." I knew it. Talking to that woman,
the city ought to close the place down. "You all about ready to go?"

"We showed those Tigers something tonight, right?"
"Thanks for the ride." "Don't you want a goodnight kiss?"
"Woo, look at that." "See you in class tomorrow."
I can't believe she did that. Maybe she likes me, too.
Lights in the kitchen. Is Mama waiting up?
"Well, look what the cat drug in. Where do you think you've been?"
"I bet he has a girlfriend. Like father, like son." "Hey kid,
you play poker?" "Maybe he plays strip poker." "You're awful."
"What are you staring at?" "Leave the boy alone." "You telling me
what to do? I know how to handle kids." "Want a drink, kid?"
"You got school tomorrow. And tell your mama to get in here,
she has company, and we want bacon and eggs."
"You tell her yourself." And get out of the room fast.
"The look on his face."

"Heart attack, that's right. Folding clothes in the bedroom.
They heard a thump and it was all over. Those poor, poor children.
And look at him, did you ever think you'd see that man cry?"
"How much longer? When will all these people ever go home?"
"Not much longer, Becky, just hang on. Aunt Mary wants you
to stay with her tonight." "I can't take much more."

"Brace yourself, here comes Granny." "You poor children.
At least the boys are out on their own so they won't be a burden.
I couldn't have loved her more if she'd been one of my own."
How true. "That's how she would have wanted to go, working
right up to the end." "There's a clean handkerchief in my coat pocket.
It'll be all right." "You look so strange in a tie."
"Oh Lord, why did you take my precious Sarah?"
I will say nothing. "Be strong, brethren.
Think on the Lord, who ordereth all things."

I'll stop by for a while. Maybe take the girls for a ride.
Signs of it already. How he looks at them, especially Becky.
Some night when he comes home drunk. Why not. Hates her too. Intelligent.
The girls? Running? "Don't you ever come back. Ever."
Drunk as a skunk, holding some kind of stick.
Running after them. "I'll give you what for, you little bitches."
Screaming. Slam on the brakes. Yank open the door, start running.
Grab his arm. Stick goes flying down in the ditch.
Right to the jaw. Never expected it from me. Smash to the chest. Nose.
Junior maybe, no more, he's married now, it's not you he'll hit.
You're strong but you're stinko. I don't even feel it. But you do.
Face down in the mud. One kick. "Don't cry, girls.
You never have to go back, never." That was the end of that.

WEASELS RIPPED MY FLESH

Down there in hell I was screaming with all the rest,
You should have heard me when weasels ripped my flesh,
Of all the women I've known her loving was the best—
it's funny, my wife doesn't like heavy metal.
Did I tell you we're having a baby? December.
Someday I'll write a country song—my serious work
is more what you might call country-folk—that everyone
who wears fringe and sequins will want to record.
Oh, Mama, Mama, I'm feeling so blue,
My girlfriend left me, and my truck died too.
Being Jewish, I can relate to that. Oh, and I'll include
at least one relative who's passed on—they love that.
But I have trouble with the words, I'm really a melody man.
I still sing in some of the Austin clubs—Austin!
how does a guy from Brooklyn end up in Austin?
Friendship, lust, chance, the usual reasons.
What a city. The cabbies—like me, I was a cabbie there—
are all bluegrass musicians who bone up on the Pre-Socratics
while they're waiting at the airport. Next thing I know,
boom, no more ponytail, no granny glasses, no gold earring,
here I am, regional troubleshooter for a big corporation,
I only show up when there's something wrong, major wrong,

they called me the angel of death. What a blast.
One day I handed 135 people their pink slips.
"Thank you very much for your services, here's two weeks' pay,
your desk is being emptied, goodbye." One hundred and
thirty-five times. And now I'm watching myself
turn into this incredibly anal-retentive asshole,
call a psychiatrist! But it's fun, the changes you go through
if you let them happen. My clients seem to confide in me,
it's not like I'm really a lawyer, well I'm part lawyer,
part father, part priest. They look to me for advice
to help them salvage their entire lives. I'd say "part rabbi,"
but no one in Texas has ever heard of Jews,
they just think I'm from New York and talk funny.
But what I really wanted to ask you was,
I have this great idea for a short story.
Dead relatives invade your dreams, begging for money.
How do you like it? A poem? No, not a poem, a short story.
Maybe you could help me with the structure, a little symbolism
here and there, et cetera. I figure it's good for a thousand words.
Would you look at me in this suit and no facial hair?
I mean I'm even wearing a vest, but the big guys like it
and my wife assures me I look terrific.
How do you write a short story, anyway?

NEOPHILIA

Saxophone stops, keyboard takes over. Saxophone wanders to a table—"Hey, Matt, Rachel!" "Great solo, man!"—keyboard, drums, bass, they don't miss him. He *was* the song, they were only following him, but who needs him? The song goes on, why, it'd go fine if he dropped dead before the finale. Lay down your solo, the next man lays down his. Not much without the group, but hell, the group's only whoever's sitting in tonight. And if you like this bassman, you should hear the other one when he bows *sul ponticello* (look it up, baby) and you spill your beer laughing. It's about time for that drummer to cut loose—let the keyboard pile up those sweet little thirds and sixths, makes you so melancholy, makes you know how good it is to feel blue, but wham! that's what's waiting for you! that's what I got waiting for you! and don't you forget it. 'Bout ready to put it all together again, saxophone quick-kissing that Amazon blonde, and look at trumpet man! He's set down his drink, and he's perched like a flamingo, flamingo in corduroy, trumpet under his left arm, right hand (it's the right leg he's standing on) with the palm back toward us, and tucked in by his thumb is a half-smoked cigarette. And what do you know, they're all back in the circle, playing together. Nobody wants the song to end, everyone's playing flat, not going anywhere near that tonic note. My girlfriend and I are laughing—now they're mocking us—our laughs coming out of their horns! Didn't know that sax could hold the note so long. Man, you were terrific. What was that one called? Don't tell me you have to go look in the notebook! "Neophilia." That's right—you play it, nobody has to know what it means.

FOR PAT GRAY

Green pesto, fresh bay scallops, and a Rhenish wine;
for going out, a hat of blue straw, broad-brimmed,
dress of dark blue sprigged with flowers:
found and shaped and assembled like a line
effortlessly expressing a thought.
Your pilgrimage led here, sans saint, sans deity, sans acolyte:
the bedroom yours (shared kitchen) and an overhead fan:
rowhouse in a city where poets come to read
and pictures are hung on display: where pediment and architrave
sing out to Greece, and strangers, occasionally,
to each other: black hair turning gray,
virility whitening into wisdom; or slenderly, collar askew,
trudging off in the dull brown of youth. It is your love
you would have them give, blossoms of living water
flung from the fountain tree. The words you seek
are the words already spoken: you have told me often
how the teacups had roses on them, and the lady
poured cream in them, and she was very old;
how you clung to the arch then bestrode the keystone;
how the woman struck and struck at the bedstead,
reddening her palms; how the only sound
was the raindrops tapping the catalpas;
how through the slow dark across the harem mosaics
the candles moved, fixed on the back of tortoises;
limbs were bare, and the Dipper hung inverted
in the winter sky; how the words were held to the light
till they exploded in a sapphire blaze;
how we ceased sculling, the boat hovered over the brown water,
the first voice from the footpath said, "In Plato's day,"
and the stag never stopped feeding.

AFTER A YEAR

Although it is still possible, in the afternoon,
to pause for tea, steeping the Earl Grey or lapsang souchong,
setting out Scottish shortbread on a lacquer tray,
even after a year it is not natural, the single cup,
fragile English bone rimmed with gold.
Each day she must re-die. He finds her
in the books, the figured rug, the chiming clock,
the chalumeau register of Brahms' clarinet;
reason says, she is gone, so he lets her disappear;
he sips the smoky liquid, till at last the warm walls,
paneled in cherry, enclose only emptiness.
Outside, spring is the color of willows; her snapdragons
bloom; gourds hang for the purple martins.
This, he thinks, submerging the teapot in soapy water,
is what many others have lived: the vast expanse
of kitchen, rooms that return to silence.
The next day, in the cove, on the old loop road,
he sees for the first time a yellow trillium;
even at noon a pair of yearling fawns
lope over the asphalt into the deeper trees.
The last time it was autumn, almost twilight,
and drizzling; the tops of the Smokies were clouded.
In the meadow the deer were grazing like cattle. She laughed
when he said the groundhog looked like a bag lady.
Driving the freeway: where he used to go to escape.
Smallest of all are the secret sweetmeats that
"helped him through": memoirs of the English pederasts;

the girls who flirted; the woman who rubbed her breasts against him
on the moonlit terrace. In his favorite chair
he sits, smoking a cigarette. The stars are out; he can just
see Jupiter over the trees. She lay in the hospital bed,
fevered and gasping for breath. That is the woman
he mourns; she spent her youth well to make her.
Tomorrow again the sun will waken him uncompanioned.
Life, the old drag queen, takes off her wig, loosens her headband,
revealing a wrinkled little man, ugly and silly.

END OF CHAPTER

Things are drawing to a close, or even more
there's a sense of looking around for the people we knew,
and we aren't there. It's not like moaning when
a green glass tower soars over the old train station
with the vaulted ceiling, the one you stared up at
until you were dizzy—we can handle the grander displacements—
it's the self and brother self we counted on, the fading away
of which reveals that we did believe in heaven,
continuator of elysian earth, we of the round table
knocking together goblets of white wine, and hearing
that divinest of sounds, poets' laughter. Some changes
are clearly for the better: no more can a sunward turn
of obsidian hair, glistening in emerald sea-froth,
unsinew us; no more, when obsidian eyes spark cruel,
the impulse to fly street-downward. Our idols
we have beaten into plowshares, and tilled some furrows
in this thin red clay. The problem's having gained our own souls
only to see all else float centripetally away,
forever lost, unless the weighty universe unspool
and we run backwards into ignorance till we're
sucked into the womb. Yet I have known
angelic beings possess us on cool March days,
walk where azaleas bloom, magenta, watermelon;
dawn sprints over low hills to join us on the heights:
cloud-mastery's common—friends, let us ride:
and the tongues of flame we spoke in lighted the city,
the multitudes awaited us in the agora:
not that they did, but that they could, were going to.
A chapter closes when what's set down so desultorily
admits no stragglers; like the pink river dolphin,

flexes on its own vertebrae. Come, flex we must
and straighten, burst into sunlight, submerge into
blue-brown murk, and sound our way upriver
till we reach the source, confluence of jungle rains and mountain snows.

HOW I WROTE IT

What the goddamn hell are you talking about, boy,
I never did one thing in my life on account of a theory—
look here: do you breathe theory? do you piss theory? do you fuck theory?
When I was living in Paris with Olga, if you've read me
you know about Olga, Polish whore and a damn good one,
claimed to be a Russian countess, that was her theory,
but she forgot she was a countess, even forgot she was a whore,
she liked it so much you see, opened her legs, dark thick hair,
rich-cunted—one point I will make for your tape recorder,
you can't be an artist without a sense of smell,
nights when I'd stagger home to Olga, I'd stop in the alley
and get a whiff of the beer, the piss, rotting vegetables,
some nights vomit, before I hauled upstairs and put it to her,
a woman who made use of a man's efforts,
not like that Japanese whore, she's in one of the books too,
who started chewing an apple when I was ready to explode.
So I'd give her the kind of fucking she was meant for
and afterwards sometimes I'd go to the typewriter buck naked
and start writing till she bitched about the noise
though more than once she fell asleep and honked like a flight of geese
but she'd bitch so I'd open a notebook and while she slept,
on summer nights the windows open and she lay there naked asleep

the covers tangled down at her knees till I wouldn't know
if I were writing with my pen or my cock, I'd use
whatever tool I needed. There were no answers
because there were never any questions. If you write,
you don't need answers. That's where you fellows go wrong.
You need books and paper and food and cunt and drink
and that's it. By daybreak there'd be pages of Olga in the typewriter,
pages of Olga in the notebook, and squirming in the bed
she'd be rubbing the yellow muck out of her big cow eyes.
Pages of Olga, and growing up in Baltimore,
the train ride to Marseille in the dead of winter,
Kontarsky and the pimples on his ass, the baptistery doors in Florence.
And I bought this great roll of wrapping paper
from a butcher shop, and on it I wrote plans, ideas, images.
Then I hung these scrolls of wrapping paper on the walls,
all around me were the books I was going to write.
Olga would have preferred pictures of milkmaids,
things she could sell for whiskey when times were bad.
The novel, how to write the novel, I heard that guff
in *caves*, bars, cafés, from writers who drank when
they should have been writing, and some, as Prescott said,
who wrote when they should have been drinking.

Art, Prescott went on and on about art, significant form,
he and his nancy-boy friends over from Oxford.
You mean writing, I said? Writing means getting your hands dirty,
writing means getting filthy all over. Holy men like dirt.
A holy man told me that once. Gurudev, surely you've heard the name.
Gurudev told me that in my room, Anneke's room actually,
I was living with Anneke then, she had a razor scar that long
across her left cheek where a crazy pimp cut her,
and the damnedest thing was, it made her sexier than before.
Every writer in Paris wanted to bang her, and a lot of them did.
One evening Gurudev was sitting cross-legged on the floor
and I decided to try it too, turned out I was a natural at it,
and Anneke got mad and pitched one of her crazy fits,
she could throw fits the way sows piss, so she was raving about men,
what pigs they were, how life was *merde* and God was a wad of snot.
Before I could swear at her, Gurudev leaned toward her, grinned,
and said, "I couldn't agree more!" Even Anneke had to laugh at that,
although she had absolutely no sense of humor and was drunk,
if he hadn't been a holy man she'd have ripped off his cotton pajamas,
damn near did it anyway—if a vixen in heat trapped in quicksand
could laugh, that was how she barked and howled with laughter.
Then she calmed down, tried to sit cross-legged and fell over backwards.

Gurudev taught some of his chanting, and I was inspired to sing
"Don't Sit Under the Apple Tree with Anyone Else but Me,"
which Anneke thought was funny, and clapped her hands like a baby,
then I sang "I'll Take You Home Again, Kathleen" like an Irish tenor,
which sounds like when you begin to sing, someone grabbed your balls
and twisted. Gurudev giggled. Indian holy men have fine giggles.
That night I explained to Gurudev how to be a writer. What was it
you said to me earlier, something about the form of the novel having failed
so that only the not-novel could be the novel? Horseshit!
Horseshit! It's the volcano inside you that has to erupt.
The lava doesn't care where it burns. If the book is bleeding chunks,
so is life. The blood lets you recognize the source.
What became of Anneke? What happened when she was with me
is in the books. After that, who knows? Now Prescott,
Prescott jumped into the Seine and hit his head on a piling.
He was in a coma for months and two of the nuns
fell in love with him. Then he recovered. Young man,
could your generation satisfy a whore? I doubt it.
I knew how to live with the grime, you see.
The grime on a tenement is as beautiful as a sunrise.

SUNBATHING IN SYRACUSE

The old men were sunbathing in the northern city.
Their cooler was full of beer and cream sodas.
The white sun felt good on their bellies.

Their beach towels were spread on a rise near the brick water tower.
The young had written their words on the tower,
who had been there, who was in love with whom.

Occasionally the men would look across the city
to the low blue hills. The chessboard was unfolded,
but they had not yet begun.

They spoke together of the latest theory, vacuum genesis,
the field for God becoming less and less,
how from nothing the elements all at once arose,

exploding to make time and space and light.
The one subject of which they never spoke
hovered between them, the son who chose

not to live, gunshot through the back of the throat.
If the one could only speculate that his own strength
was the rock on which a weak bark shattered,

the more objective, who had lost only the love for a wife,
could consider the longer perspectives, the act beaded in a bit of
microscopic code, or in a plenitude of worlds

the probabilities working out the same.
A girl, thin with stringy long brown hair,
didn't know they gazed at her, her face

bruised with a bliss she lifted to her boyfriend,
not good enough for her, they agreed. Her eyes shone
as if to call to her embrace the sum of all things to come.

The old men drank their sweet sodas and set up the chessboard,
arranging their white and black,
enjoying the light and coolness of the summer air.

AENEAS

He goes out to the garage each morning,
carrying his lawn chair, and sets it up
at the back, half turned toward the new Buick.
It's cool there, is all he says.
The son learns not to watch from the house.
His father wants to plant lilacs;
put some color in the yard, he always explains.
Ten minutes digging and the coughing gets him.
In the evening he stacks his chair by the kitchen door.
At dinner the stories he tells are of war,
Army bases in Texas, amphibious landings in Italy.
His little grandson loves him.
After a few beers, the old man wavers up the stairs.
Aeneas is not there to carry him.
He listens from the next room,
remembering what must be left undone,
what words cannot be spoken.

REVELATION

To pray that the love of Christ come down,
each morning, and break his fast in the silent kitchen,
marriage a vocation to which he was not called—
over the toast he reviewed the heads of his sermon:
Christ on the cross, his agony, how that was his love;
each of us on a cross, let that be our love.
How little they sensed the godhead within,
the boys who hung out in the park,
the one, greasy hair and a gold earring,
who got in his car. Heartbreaking that one so young
had seen so much of the world, and that the worst,
profaning in casual words the highest power.
Which made it all the more touching, the look on his face
when he saw the room in the basement, for once
his own room. Rake leaves and fire the furnace,
learn how a human being could live. When the boy
came to him, spreading his arms like angel wings,
what could he say but take, this is my body.
Clumsy and hurtful and sweet. Transfigurations of the days,
hills going russet and burnished yellow,
spider mums in a silver pitcher, the stranger in the shower,
and all, all, surrendered up to the one
who turns thinnest grape juice to holiest wine.
He woke early one morning and knew: the greater the love,
the greater the burden. Christ lived to show us that.
The boy still slept, innocent of the Lord. Belt scars
from parent or client. The parsonage ladies finally agreed
he was a Christian project. No interest in school,
but that would come. Hair shorter, the earring gone,

he would talk sometimes to the neighbors' children.
If he retreated to his basement room
and played the radio loud, that was normal.
To hold everything together, the choir's need for new robes,
the deacon with Parkinson's disease, the prayers to be shown
the will of the savior—expecting the boy to return the feelings
of a grown man—but those eyes and blunt fingers,
such age in them. After the session meeting one afternoon,
he drove up and opened the garage door. The radio
loud inside. "Ray?" Not on the first floor.
A whimpering from below. He descended the stairs.
Still some smell of the damp. The boy crouched near the furnace,
a wild look, surely on some kind of drug. "Ray?"
Weeping. Stains on the shirt. He made himself enter the room.
Precious Jesus, the blood. The little girl, her body
broken on the bed. The electric blanket, soaked through.
What money he had, fifty dollars, and the key to the Olds,
he couldn't not give him that. The boy gunned out of the driveway
and knocked down the mailbox. He sank by the window,
trying to name all the authorities who must be notified.

OPUS POSTHUMOUS

As the northers sweep down after icing the Panhandle,
dumping snow on the dry central beds,
but then bumping against the hills around Boerne,
losing force after spit-freezing the roads,
and leaving the south, once the overall gray diminishes,
only a weird blue cold,
so too after the death, Dolores, the storm weakening
and regathering out toward the gulf,
you will on a winter morning, orange dawn outlining the conifers,
look out through clear glass at the bell tower.
Lesson the first, to look out. There is no more inside.
Down to the candor of bone, crooked branches bending
before the wind. From now on, nothing spectacular will happen.
The grackle's tail slips sideways as it walks into the wind.
The land is level here, and the palm trees, blasted to straw
by the cold, hang far from the sea. Out into the cold you walk,
unresisting, the electric air blue as you leave the apartment behind.
No bell resounds from the brick tower on the single hill,
and you sit at the dry fountain by the paths
across which no one is moving. Cottonwood, cedar,
and Chinese tallow branch over the convent wall.
Lesson the second, to look back. What you recall
is no longer personal. Your memories are not your fate,
having no structure. Here's one: he stormed to the basement,
you not crying; synthesizers and bells, loud, from below;
you turned over pages, fingering red rock and heat
and painted sunsets. Another: she looked up at you
with his eyes, afraid of him. And this one: you pregnant and sick
on the picnic, light rain falling, he stroked the back of your neck
with the back of his hand. The black figure you see

is a lightning-charred corpse: one touch of the wind
and the ashes crumple. Lesson the next,
that this death is perfect freedom. Cut the strings on memory:
sandhill cranes crossing a pale moon.
In the cloister the nuns pray for such lightness.
Like the point on the horizon where only
a few minutes ago the morning star glimmered,
impersonally you rise from the fountain edge,
invisible now in this whiteness, this dazzling light.

TAKE FIVE

"This time I don't want to see quite so much imagination.
None of that indicated stuff, don't even try any scene stealing
if you know what's good for you. There's no scene to steal,
have you got that? The whole point is that there's no audience,
get rid of the idea of an audience by looking away from each other.
No, not looking away from each other—not looking.
If you happen to catch someone's eye when you turn around,
okay, don't act like you've seen your agent,
but don't make quote unquote eye contact. You're not acting here.
There is not where we do the heavy duty Marlon Brando
'I'm acting, I'm acting' routine. Try not to fall in the water, Sam,
we don't have all night, and I'd like to get the effect
of those lights across the river before the ballgame's over
and they suddenly switch off in mid-scene, all right it's not a ballpark,
I don't want to know. No, this time we're not cueing the record,
total silence. Maybe there'll be some smoky jazz underneath
when it hits the theaters, all I've seen our esteemed composer do
is shovel my hard-earned money up his nose, so for now
assume it will be silence. Sam, Robert, hearing aids in place?
Under the hair more, Robert, we hired you to look sexy. Good.
Don't move till you hear me whisper. Jocelyn, pull the hat brim down
so we can see more of the ribbon. Look out at the houseboat
and say your line, I know it's really a workboat,
but say your line anyway, darling, half the audience
will think it really is a houseboat, and the rest will think
I'm a bloody genius for having you say it's a houseboat

when it isn't, so please, beautiful, just say the line
as artlessly as you did the last time. And Kip, your fans
have a whole movie to see if they love you without a beard,
your profile is not the focal point of this scene.
I'm more interested in your Hawaiian shirt, you want the truth.
Houseboat, can you hear me? You know when the light's
supposed to go off? Places, everyone. Keep the onlookers
back behind that rope, and if one of them makes a sound,
I will break and cut everything breakable and cuttable.
Are we nervous, kids? Are we going to screw up again?
Action! Count to five, Sam, then lean on the piling.
Hold it and look out." Isosceles triangle, Sam at the point,
Jocelyn and Kip on the bench, against Sam-Kip-Robert,
the long scalene. Camera low enough to catch the far shore,
lights still diffusing in the haze. They'll be able to feel
how muggy it is. That planet's in the viewfinder, reddish tint,
must be Mars. ("Now, Robert, the line you improvised.")
"I've done some of my best writing on trains."
("Don't move a muscle, Sam. We know you're taking it all in.")
Goddamn Kip, there's his profile, no it's right,
his instincts were right, he should look down the dock at Robert.
Sam and Jocelyn don't. Let the words die out
like the notes at the end of a phrase. Count thirty,
don't rush, don't rush. Yes. "Someday I'm going to
live on a houseboat." She's caught it, leaving the men free
to respond or not as they like. ("Nod, Sam.")

Four pairs of eyes on the boat ("Out!") and the light goes out.
Outtake of breath. Kip: "That must be our cue to go."
("Hesitate, Sam. Look at Kip, then Robert.") If you stayed,
one of you would have to speak of your love for each other,
and tell how love works to silence you before each other,
ready to spin you back to the too familiar,
giving only new loss for comfort. Someone would have to speak
of the beauty of night and moving water, and another
would briefly give rein to death-fears, whereupon
the fourth, the one whose voice had not been heard,
would call up those ichor-veined selves
who for briefest spells seem almost capable of divinity—
my God! was that a heron? that dark shape?—we got it,
we'll slow down that part of the tape almost to stillness—
there's Sam, he turns and squints and can't make it out
and it's flown away. ("Move, Robert.") Your walk, we see
the tough fluidity you've mastered, it touches us
that you wanted to. Move, Kip, keep the reserve in your eyes.
Move, Sam, angle your way unwillingly out of the frame.
And finally, move, Jocelyn, least involved and most absolving,
the last thing we see is the rose ribbon on the brim.
"Cut! Print it! Not bad, boys and girls, you managed to remember
your lines this time. Pack up this crapola on the double,
then two blocks up the street and we do the scene
where they think they hear a cat up a tree.
Spare me the kvetching. Most of the night is still ahead of us."

PART II

The Revenge by Love

(1995)

A FEW LAST THINGS

He had morning tea with the housekeeper,
a kind, loud woman whose braids
kept coming undone. She talked to him about Jesus;
he said they'd made their peace. She looked unsure.
Why do you want to reach heaven? he teased.
Even if the streets were gold, you'd still want to scrub them.
He'd imagined leaving a testament,
a parchment scroll bearing a secret doctrine
to kindle the initiates, or a plain speech
where "tree" would mean tree and "light" only light,
or words steely with wisdom, polished epigrams
compressing a lifetime's understanding. Wrongheaded again.
He was old, that was all, and sometimes he wrote.
He'd learned to step carefully out to the screen porch.
His wife's African violets still hung from hooks;
he made the housekeeper take care of them.
She said she'd like to get rid of them, those fuzzy leaves
gave her the creeps. Cardinals drank from the birdbaths
his wife insisted he build the year she died.
Birds seemed to fit their world better than humans.
His wife dead, the friend he used to argue philosophy with
dead. He was no longer impressed by the set of meanings
he'd argued for, true enough but small. He needed
to think of his parents so they wouldn't go unremembered,
how they sailed from Poland, seasick every day,
and Natalia, speechless after her stroke,
whose low-pitched laugh he'd fallen in love with.
What good it did for a man, loving a beautiful woman:
his stride quickened, his work flowed, his sense of the world

enlarged, well worth his wife's suffering.
The housekeeper disliked his daughter; she even
mimicked how her mouth was drawn to one side
as she recited a catalogue of mistreatment
and complained of the sons she hadn't brought to see him.
She'd liked laying her dark hair against his arm,
an affectionate child. What he had was
another morning of sunlight and a breeze
stirring the acid-blue hydrangeas. A notebook by the chair
and a pen he could still hold. The revenge by love.

ZORAMEL

The light through the chink in the curtains still woke him
after he'd slept with his best friend's girl.
He'd reach for a cigarette or head for the shower,
keeping the usual routine. Only once
did he start the morning with Scotch—
that, he could tell, was pretty useless.
When he didn't have classes he worked on his novel,
just notes so far about Zoramel, land of high mountains,
where the Piliashtili fled a century ago
when the usurper struck. They were highly evolved,
the Piliashtili, in matters of telepathy,
valuable for those who live on mountains.
He didn't much like her, that was how it started,
the way she was on-again, off-again tore Roland apart.
Why couldn't she see that? She thought dinner was a good idea,
the two who cared most for Roland should get to know each other.
He told her about Zoramel as they walked up the ridge,
how the most sacred ritual was the ceremony of high waters.
The priests kept vigil when the waterfalls began to melt,
and everyone threw dried flowers into the gorge
so that the meadows would bloom again.
She insisted he include something funny in his book,
a forgetful magician or a freckled tomboy who swore.
He picked some chicory for her lapel;
Piliashtili kings dressed in chicory-blue.
The clairvoyant among them lived with the branching of paths,
foreknowledge of possible futures. Glimpses, images,
a banquet held by torchlight, a dungeon. A first-born son
who might share the taint of witch-blood. Not always knowing
when the event would happen or whether the potion drunk,

the quest accepted, fulfilled or annihilated the vision.
They were the ones right for each other, he on top of her,
hands interlocked, he slowly licking her nipples.
Roland was much too old for her. He himself
was now Roland, touching with Roland's fingers,
sensing with Roland's nerves. Her brown eyes and oval face.
The white marks of her bikini straps, she was so small.
They were lovers, she was his destiny! Or they could be
casual lovers, clasping with more laughter than passion:
he gave himself to her, whatever she desired of him.
They had brought this moment into the world and could not
unmake it. Afterward she wept. Since he was the only one there,
his responsibility was to hold her, stroke her hair,
murmur sounds. He was glad she was willing to stay the night,
though she crept to one side of the bed. He still
felt her against him whenever he tried to turn over.
What the book needed was plot. The young prince
could restore the fortunes of the Piliashtili,
that was almost a given, and would probably fall in love.
He hadn't worked out how it would happen. Maybe the villains
could be shape stealers frightened of the sun.
The prince would journey through Zoramel, with or without
a magician. Roland was no help, he didn't like fantasy novels,
and he was obsessed with her, he thought she'd been unfaithful.
He could scarcely teach, let alone work on his thesis.
She hadn't told Roland. But wouldn't she?
Would she be able not to? He found himself telling Roland
about Memnor, Isle of the Glassy Lake, where stood a sacred grove,
and whatsoever was done in that grove, even murder,
was instantly annulled after the deed. The victim

you hacked to pieces stood up and walked out with you.
The prince was under strict instructions not to enter that wood.
The Scotch was making Roland look tearful. If Roland cried,
he would be forced to comfort him.

POLITICS

Campari and soda? You've never tried it?
Why then, my dear, you must. Rather a surprise,
your turning up like this, but a most pleasant one,
I assure you. Why yes, of course I recall last night—
a most agreeable chat—asking you to stop by sometime.
One likes being taken at one's word. What was it
we were talking about? Politics! No wonder I have
such a headache. The topic requires so much Scotch.
Or, in this case, Campari. What do you think?
Keep sipping, you may develop a taste for it.
A good drink to order at one of your regular haunts.
Bartenders usually remember, and lovely conversations begin.
Was I carrying on about Reagan? Sometimes I remark how brilliant he was
just to watch people blanch. And we really discussed
my own political career? Speaking of abortions,
which we weren't. I wouldn't call it a sacrifice,
the term sounds rather grand. A conscious decision, certainly.
Who knows if I could have been elected? Family tradition,
connections, inherited wealth, these have been known to help.
And my countenance was thought becoming in those days.
You're much too kind. I was quite a firebrand,
I'd have favored revolution, provided my nearest and dearest
were gunned down first. Mainly the ones who'd put up the money.
I believed blacks in the South should be treated as equals—
this was back when we in the North thought we set an example,
long before your time. Since I was of the right class,
and possessed of a certain wit and charm, it was felt
I could help bring it off. As for foreign affairs,

they're part of a gentleman's education.
But the life wasn't for me, you see. Because the other life was.
The compromise didn't seem all that bad; the fact is
I've always gotten on well with women—I even like
sleeping with them. But not to be able to spend one's vacation on Bali
with a youth slightly underage—not reprehensible there,
I assure you, and nothing to what the late J. Edgar used to do
in his hideaway near San Juan. Those rumors are entirely true.
Perhaps you'll have trouble imagining how repressed we were—
how repressed they were, I can fairly say—though the mighty
found ways of indulging their tastes. A high prelate of the church—
you'd recognize the name—perhaps not, since you were
a Jehovah's Witness—offered to take me along to his favorite
brothel, male, it goes without saying. Out of his robes
and into a suit the vulgarity of which would not have disgraced
a tourist from Dubuque, and off we went. The madam,
male again, cooed like a maître d' when a film star enters.
The madam was Flatbush Jewish with a lovely Harvard accent. We sat
in red velvet chairs and played cribbage while our churchly Casanova
went off to spread his gospel and partake of the brotherhood of man
with his usual playmate. Black, I believe. Oh no, I merely
chaperone the clergy in bordellos and tell tales afterward.
But as the padre observed when he was once again
clothed in the robes of chastity and goodness, say what I might,
who would believe me? How would a politician react to that?
That's what we expect politicians to do, have opinions and react.
They shouldn't possess too many ideals, but at least a glittering few.
We don't like cynics, rightly, I think, and distrust

too much intelligence. Considering how McNamara and his clever lads
ran the Vietnam War by computer printout, again perhaps rightly.
Would you like to hear my plan for world peace? This would actually work.
Every day after lunch, without fail, every world leader would be
required to masturbate. There'd be no more war. The UN could supervise.
It would have done Margaret Thatcher a world of good, not to mention
the old boys in Beijing. But who listens to reason these days?
One's best ideas go for naught, and the world limps along somehow.
What a very nice idea you had, dropping by, but you look
terribly warm. Perhaps if I simply undo this button.

AND PART OF HER ANUS IN DALLAS

She'd come to a new city, Dallas this time, but all the systems were already in place, everything was connected with everything else. Except that she wasn't, and everyone would expect her to be.

She wrote out her resolutions: Never wear a tux. Never go out with a woman who's wearing a tux. No waitresses, no cashiers, no gym teachers.

The restaurants she went to played songs that were supposed to bring back memories. They didn't. But then she had the memory of hearing those songs in the restaurants.

During Beth and Muriel's party she suddenly got up and said, "I am a woman. I have a right to control my body. I make intelligent choices. I am in charge of my life." Then sat back down.

When you were with someone, that person would always say things and expect you to respond. It was as if they expected a natural ebb and flow, one thing following another, like a play where the actors said their lines and gave each other their cues. But this was real life, wasn't it, no one had written any dialogue.

One of the better paranoid theories was that big business encouraged the breakup of relationships because it doubled the market for basic consumer goods.

Funny how everyone wanted to see patterns. Take the thing with Dan. Muriel asked was she trying to prove something. Mother thought it was her salvation. Karla thought she'd gone crazy. Whereas she and Dan saw it as more of an interlude. It didn't really mean much of anything except that it happened.

Even some of the there's-no-such-thing-as-reality gang probably changed their minds on the downward plunge from the Empire State Building.

She'd open the door and Judy would be shrieking *Do you have any idea what time it is There's no catfood You forgot to buy catfood It's that nurse from the party I saw you looking at her.* Or bayberry candles on the table, chilled wine, dark red roses.

Oh for the days when they drank herbal tea and listened to Phoebe Snow.

Beth and Muriel had been together six years. Amy and Fran had been together four years. Violet and Marie had been together eighteen years. Phyllis and Denise had been together three months.

She turned to the last page: "Her auburn locks blew gently in the warm summer breeze. Brittany had never imagined such happiness was possible. As Chance enfolded her in his strong arms, she knew that the whole future lay open before them."

THE WAITER

For the last time he put on the frilled white shirt,
the black pants, tied on the apron with deep pockets.
He gathered the slick white menus and greeted
the early arrivals. He smiled the accustomed smile
as he took the drink orders, suggested the blackened redfish
and ground fresh pepper on the Boston lettuce.
An older couple exclaimed at the scalloped butter rosettes.
In the past he had made up stories about the people he served,
the young husband who wouldn't look at his wife,
afraid to reveal so much love; the woman who ate alone
reading Agatha Christie. He had learned
to maintain a proper retreat; that was more loving.
All he wanted tonight was to freshen the iced teas,
to talk about bread pudding and Kahlua cheesecake.
When he moved his lumbering frame back to the kitchen,
placing the orders for chicken with artichoke hearts,
none of the others lingered to speak, Bill with another story
about the new baby, or Ron, not high tonight, who'd said
he looked like a big teddy bear and put his hands on him.
Just as well get used to the discomfort others would feel,
how the monk's robe would mean he was not the same,
himself not a body like other bodies, the self withering in prayer.
As in work. The woman in the green dress had changed her mind
and wanted dessert. Certainly. More of his tables filling up,
tonight would be hectic. Then sometime after eleven
he would pull the door shut behind him, perhaps with
no more than the usual goodbyes, and begin his journey
to a room with white walls and a hard bed
where he could be nothing and God could be always.

DIRT

You think your place is a mess? You should have
seen Frankie's. I never told you about Frankie?
We go back a long way. He was the only one who didn't
think it was weird for a Texan to chew bouillon cubes
or read Camus on the school bus. We argued a lot
about Angst and what kind of car we'd buy
if we had five hundred bucks. Frankie,
this is typical, wanted a Chevy Vega even though
I told him the aluminum around the engine fell apart
after ten thousand miles. We were at this car lot, see,
and straight as a shot Frankie heads for a Vega
whose insides were completely burned out.
It figured, it really did. And dirt:
he had a system about dirt. Wait long enough
and someone else will clean it for you.
Usually me—you noticed I'm kind of compulsive?
Once, this was one of the times he was in college,
what did I find by his mattress but a rubber
in a coffee cup. Used. Oh, but things were worse
after he got married the second time. She was pregnant
by someone else and, this is hard to believe, messier than Frankie.
I've seen everything mixed up in stacks on the floor,
steak knives, bills, dirty diapers, dog food,
the library was on his ass about Kierkegaard,
and from the street you could see the grow lights
for his marijuana plants, even though the cops
had busted him twice. Frankie had a good heart, though,
he put up with me all these years, and he took in this old dog
who'd been hit by a car. One afternoon, he may have had

his sociology degree by then, I go over to his place.
The door's open, and Frankie's asleep, blanket
pulled up to his chin except for his long bushy beard,
and sticking up from under the bed, he has a bed by then,
are the stiff legs of that poor old dog. I shake him:
"Frankie, Frankie, the dog's dead." "He's just sleeping."
"Frankie, the dog is *dead*." He went right back to sleep.
Then there were the times we smoked dope
when Frankie would say he couldn't understand
why there was so much evil, since the whole world
was only inside his head—a scary idea. We lost touch
when I started teaching, he said I'd sold out.
Then a couple of years ago I heard he was working
in a bank. Then I heard he was delivering pizzas.
I was dating an ex-girlfriend of his, real pretty,
not as pretty as you—oh yes, you like it—and we thought about
ordering a pizza. When Frankie arrived we'd be standing there
stark naked. But we never did.

A LITTLE HUNGER

Not the puffy beef tacos, her absolute favorites,
though the Iranian owner attempted to make them
as fat-free as possible. No refried beans ever ever
so chalupas were out. Chicken fajitas? They could
order chicken fajitas for two and she could let Eric
eat more than half. They could get corn tortillas
but Eric really preferred flour, well so did she
for that matter, and he liked beef better than chicken,
so maybe the combo fajitas for two and she could coax him
to eat some of the chicken. She'd limit herself on
chips and salsa and leave most of the guacamole (so good!
and so fattening!) and all of the sour cream (she could be
strong) for Eric. He'd suggested Mexican tonight because
he knew how much she loved it. He liked pleasing her
and wanted her to be pleased. He was close, he was closer
than anyone ever had been, to proposing, and if—
she wasn't going beyond if—he did, he'd expect her to say yes.
She would say yes. She'd given little hints she would,
like when Barbara and Raul got engaged and she said
what a neat couple they made because they were such friends
and had so much fun together, which was what she and Eric
said about themselves. She hadn't wanted to marry anyone
before law school and in law school who had time
to do anything but read cases and order in pizza? Mushrooms
and pepperoni with extra cheese. Yum. At work
she could exist on microwave popcorn (unsalted,
unbuttered, as much as she wanted) and diet Pepsi.
Eric said he loved her figure, which was sweet, but
did anyone really love cellulite thighs? After marriage
you had to expect some weight gain (from Eric, too,

who was a chicken-fried steak kind of guy, she'd cook it
and have to eat her share of it) and after a child
still more pounds but everyone expected you to diet then.
Damn, there was no way out of a margarita (as if
she needed liquor to say yes) but she could gracefully
stop at one. She'd eaten entirely too many chips
and Eric was prone to ordering chocolate desserts
she at least had to taste. If he spent the night,
and he probably would, she had his favorite
cream-filled doughnuts for breakfast, and with coffee and juice
she could get away with taking only part of a doughnut.
A little bite. Leaving him with almost all of the filling.

CAMILLE IN LUXOR:
SAINT-SAENS VISITS EGYPT, 1896

To be wakened by the croaking of frogs and peepers
in the blinding dawn—an Egyptian winter
remote from Parisian fogs, air so dry
the dust fell easily off. By noon,
white heat glowed on the river
flowing like liquid tin, and the dahabeeyahs
floated without a ripple.
Mornings he was content to observe
the half-hidden temple rising above the quay,
or look across the river to villages built of mud, where
buffaloes sank up to the shoulder dragging their yokes,
or in the marketplace to be jostled by guides,
beggars, donkey boys, Copts tattooed with crosses,
a one-eyed vendor hawking morsels of roast mutton.
Cacophonies of language, such strange perfumes.
Afternoons he would return to the houseboat or stroll
on the towpath overhung with yellow mimosas,
jot botanical notes about date palms and cycads,
or purchase the company of young fauns
to whom one was invariably kind.
And the nights! Silver light and gray shadows,
as if they were days under a spell of enchantment
when the moon rose over the hills and lit the Nile
like a softer sun. The Nubian boatmen
sang strophes of love unfulfilled,
and his telescope found stars tinged greenish and red.
He joined nocturnal excursions to Karnak
riding down long avenues of stone rams,
an Academician of sixty on a donkey,
anxious to raise his lamp to examine the wall-paintings,

profiles of gods half-bestial, histories
reduced to inscriptions and colored emblems,
then sealed in such disproportioned tombeaus.
The explorers returned to a feast by the river,
a sheep roasted whole, drums and reed flute,
dancing females, the dragoman chanting Arabic poems,
far from the Paris to which he must return,
where a young wife could neglect her duty
and a son fall dead from a window,
return with only a concerto as canopic urn
for Luxorian sounds and textures—the flapping of sails,
Ali grunting, a crocodile moving in the moonlit water—
even the thud of propellers as the steamer
carried the voyager toward home,
which no longer existed.

SUN PICTURES

Suppose we tried to recapture in photographs
our morning drive to Rochester. One year ago today.
I'd want to take pictures of the towns' names,
homage to the classical world whose virtues
would flourish again: Ithaca, so that a wanderer
will build his last dwelling by tranquil water;
Romulus, so that the wild hills will nourish
a founder of cities; Ovid, so that the native tongue
will acquire potency and wit. We'd choose
exempla of the truest American pastoral,
hundred-year oaks, brick houses with plain Doric columns,
white clapboard churches. We'd add details simply because
we liked them: the plaque for the Philomathic Library,
cornfields with signs indicating the breed:
Garst 8808. I would charge these cultivated hills
with longing, a Tennesseean's nostalgia
for green after green. We'd need shots of ourselves
as you drove through the August morning,
Cayuga Lake off to our right. You'd brought
red seedless grapes and bottles of sparkling water,
lime-flavored, passionfruit-flavored.
We said little except to confirm our sense
that at every curve the road presented significant objects,
so that the act of seeing became the act of vision.
At last our two-lane reached the highway,
reminding us we had a destination:
not illumination, but history. Your house:
kitchen of light-grained wood, dining room
hung with prints of Shakespearean actors.
You showed me the museum membership cards,

I could use your husband's. But lunch before art.
The Art Deco diner—you knew I'd love it—waitresses
capped and aproned in black and white, framed clippings
(Titanic Sinks; We Like Ike for Four More Years),
photos of stars: Bacall, Louise Brooks, Montgomery Clift.
You told me when Eastman, old and sick, killed himself,
he left a note: "Why should I wait? My work is done."
Today at noon in the Alamo Gardens, while tourists
snap pictures of each other, I remember how we
hurried under the porte-cochere, showed our cards,
ascended a hardwood staircase to the rooms where Eastman
slept and thought, turned into a brief history
of the art his genius kept giving means to.
You showed me a sepia photograph of the Louvre, off-center angle,
textures of stone, only twenty years into the art.
The sheen on the Weston pepper. "Erotic." "Funny."
Steichen's Duse, how her long neck seemed somehow
the key to tragedy. "And the fuzzy focus. Tragedy
depends on a slight blur." Muybridge, who murdered
his wife's lover, created an atlas of motion,
naked beings as noble as ancient gods.
And his Yosemite, sheer walls fringed daintily with trees,
rocks like buttresses, spires, domes, skulls, viscera.
Your favorite was Julia Margaret Cameron:
her husband sits in majesty as if from another sphere,
white hair gleaming like sea foam, hands touching
a golden chain—"O what good it does to one's soul
to go forth!" she wrote. She would have made you
one of her beautiful puritans, hair parted and coiled,
drapery pulled about to conceal your shape

so that you emerge dramatically from darkness,
a form for inwardness. She began at fifty. Fifty years
to prepare for art. The Larry Clark kept drawing me back:
scrawled across the top in capital letters,
DEATH IS MORE PERFECT THAN LIFE. His creed, the hometown
James Dean who perches on the bed with a revolver,
bare chest, slicked-back dark hair? The distance he keeps
invites the partners who'll never reach him, wildness
pressed in, as if neither body nor soul could offer
y to his x, the globe itself is inadequate.
Even death is inadequate. A card tells us
he overdosed on heroin shortly thereafter.
Or do the words provide only texture, played off against
the shape the human object takes, the image
held up against the words, the words leading back to the image?
Today by the Alamo the trees each carry a nameplate:
pecan; mescal bean. A bed of geraniums re-creates
the Lone Star flag. A gray-haired woman about sixty
hands me her Polaroid and asks if I'll take a picture.
Second honeymoon, she winks, indicating her husband,
golfing cap, walrus mustache, pale blue guayabera,
who obligingly grins. They pose stiff in front of the wall,
a sweep of oak branch behind them. "One more," she calls,
leaning against his shoulder. Already the first shot's
nearly dried into form. At Eastman House
we stopped in front of Verdi, the young Oscar Wilde,
attempting to read one expression for a final disclosure.
Freeze-frame: transfixed by the Cartier-Bresson:
I kept glancing at you. He bicycles into the sun-blur,
the French boy, passing a flight of stairs. Chance

plus vigilance plus camera equals art, I teased.
You touched my sleeve. Not chance. All elements,
you said, were pre-arranged. We'd come to the end
of our tour. These are the sun pictures I printed:
descent of the stairs. Red-gold hair.
Unadorned white linen. In the midday glare
wife and husband reclaim their camera, bid me
goodbye and walk off. I vanish from their lives.

O'Keeffe and Stieglitz

STIEGLITZ TALKING TO THE DISCIPLES, 1916

"An American art, that is what I ask of you,
an art worthy of this land, do I not have the right to ask it?
Paint your pictures and I will hang them,
I will find buyers, but they must be truly your pictures,
shall a young painter be content to mimic the Europeans?
When you have this vast continent, unexplored,
unexplored in the figurative sense, my meaning was quite clear,
the American landscape, these enormous buildings, must you
kiss a raddled whore in Montmartre to imagine yourself a painter?
But of course you're right to admire Braque and Duchamp and Kandinsky,
what do you mean, not Kandinsky, he puts emotions on canvas,
that remark was crude and uncalled for, young man,
you want to paint greatly yet you lack civilization,
think of a man like Goethe, no American can compare with him,
indeed I am not contradicting myself, never
I emphasize never do I contradict myself, but if you
cannot follow the turns of thought in civilized discourse—
Goethe I say Goethe had the romantic heart, the romantic soul
but an intellect sharp as the scientist's lens,
how dare you say, 'Oh, yes, but I am from New Jersey,'
was Weimar Weimar before Goethe made it so?
You must make of New Jersey a second Weimar,
if it is necessary to your genius you will do it, a stoa of
philosophers and artists, yourself a Goethe who goes on creating,
or learn a lesson from Ibsen, the master builder himself,
he could have stopped, he would still have been great,
but he kept quarrying and quarrying out of himself,
you speak of baring your soul in paint, is your soul
really that small, can a few paltry canvases, I am not
calling your canvases paltry, contain all of a human soul,

an Ibsen throws out soul here, soul there, and always there is more,
no matter how old or weary he goes on, no no I agree,
John Gabriel Borkman is no *Hedda*, *Hedda* we can never forget,
but he goes on, forcing himself to climb his towers and mountains,
When We Dead Awaken, and when shall we who are not dead awaken,
when shall you who are young awaken?" I sat
to one side, dressed in black, and did not speak.
My hair came loose and tumbled around my shoulders.

STIEGLITZ:
EARLY PHOTOGRAPHS OF O'KEEFFE

The fingers, poised around buttons of bone.
Eyes of an herb woman in a Chinese village.
Luxurious hair wrapped up around her head;
breasts as white and innocent as her arms.
Light glowing on white flanks.
The shadowy pubis.

>   Champagne, M'sieu? A poor girl like me
>   isn't used to such delicacies.
>   How do I look in your derby hat?
>   If I let the shirt fall open,
>   surely no one would object. I think
>   I would now like a little champagne.
>   Oh, M'sieu. M'sieu is much too kind.

In a white gown of many folds the woman stands,
her hair dark and flowing. She is ready for tragedy
and will answer to the name Andromache.
Andromache owns the fury of Clytemnestra
but will not express it. By this she comprehends
nobility. Her eyes see her child torn from her grasp
and smashed to the rocks below. The loss of a husband
is every woman's lot. You will not hear
the howls of her lamentations.

>   Here in front of a painting, my love,
>   I will pose you. Only a corner of the painting.
>   They will see this woman is an artist,
>   her work stretches out of our sight
>   but we will follow. Can't you hold still, damn it,

another plate ruined. Hold still while I make you immortal.
This is how woman looks when she creates.
No, love, I am wrong, it is you who make me immortal,
you who restore art to one whom art had renounced.
To photograph one person over many years,
the whole become one photograph of love.

Don't swear at me if you want me to model.
I could be painting instead, you old goat.
Pose me nude in January—you would.
Like this? Yes, I know the expression.
Quick, take your picture.
You can photograph me for a lifetime
and never comprehend the mystery.
But every woman should have a lover like you.
I am yours. Enter! Enter!

LAKE GEORGE

Spring: usually chilly. Lilacs opened heart-shaped leaves among the pine and white birch. Grape shoots were velvety pink. She liked to wade in the streams, hunting for cresses.

June, and the fields dotted with white daisies. Then relatives arrived, his relatives, with their children who even dared to call her Aunt Georgia, their scampering around and spying where they did not belong, sister-in-law Selma and her ankle-biting bulldog, meals that demanded family disagreements simply to announce one's presence. And his friends couldn't remain in Manhattan or leave behind Cézanne's plastic values and the proper anti-fascist position. Better to climb Prospect Mountain every day and walk through the grove of white birches.

Autumn was best for painting. Cicadas screeched in the evenings and Canada geese flew over the lake. Hillsides of sugar maples turned red. At sunrise the trunk of an old birch was bleached white, but the leaves were radiant gold. By November the sky darkened; heavy clouds drizzled. She was exhausted and pale, painted out, they had to return to the city. The mountain turned brownish-purple except for patches of evergreen.

JUDITH

She presided over the dining room,
Miss Marblehead, from a fringed scarf
atop the china closet, granting us
the favor of her royal simper
and a breast absent-mindedly exposed.
Heroine of the Hebrews indeed! As if to save her people
she only needed antimacassars for the horsehair sofa.
We dug the hole deep that night.
How the spade resounded in the hard earth,
the sweat cooled quickly on our bodies.
All three conspirators raised her high,
then let her drop.
That's earth smearing your face, milady.
Let the relatives wail at her absence—
one of their forebears had, after all, purchased her—
feigning ignorance was quite agreeable.
I could have but did not explain:
artists make the best critics.

A CONVERSATION

No, it would be quite impossible,
we are agreed. Hush, my dear,
you need not argue. Our views are identical.
You do not feel the physical craving,
I would not expect you to.
You can see, even more clearly than I,
the practical side, how our lives, our two lives,
would fracture, inevitably diminished
by increase. Think of the hours I spend
preparing the canvas, mixing each color with a separate brush.
What infant would respect those hours?
Or even the days I spend without paint,
walking by Lake George when lilacs begin to open,
or simply waiting. Cooking. Yes, I would be diverted.
The poem you wrote for me, about the woman who carries
dawn in her womb. How does that feel, I wonder?
No, I do not know. How free, and how wise,
you are, not imagining you need a son
or another daughter. No daughter of ours
would turn away from the light, from her little son,
like your poor girl, or would a child we made
be smothered by us, by a surfeit of life, or art,
which seem to be the same thing. Your photographs
will carry you forward. That is enough.
For me—swirls of azure on stark white?
A shape. That's all, merely a shape. A flower,
oh, a black iris. We will not speak of sacrifice.
Let us end this long conversation. Come to bed.

FLOWERS

1

larger than the humans who stand in front of them

2

like butterflies pinned open
or lit from within

3

fringed orchid
exploding with light at the center

4

the hollyhock's black sheen glows with red,
and the larkspur, blue crystals of larkspur!

5

the white trumpet-flower
all its curves are hard-edged

6

the shape at the top of the bleeding heart
an apple dipped in ashes

7

a ribbon of light
through the green corn

dark leaves, light veins
reaching in opposite directions

morning by morning
a drop of dew slips down the veins
to pool in the sheath's dark center

8

if you think the stamens and pistils are phallic
the lip-shaped petals a vulva
I don't

9

they're cheaper than models
and they don't move

10

the large white flower with the golden heart
is something I have to say about white

11

petals of the white rose unfold
like a drama at Epidaurus

12

the dark spider at the heart of the scarlet poppy

13

purple iris
tonguelike, velvety, purplish-gray petals
uncurling into blackness

14
when the painter is unafraid
the result is calmness

15
stripes of the jack-in-the-pulpit
this time the interior all black
a thin stalk of white rises from the plump candle

the final variation the most abstract
only the jack
against a doorway of white

OBSERVATIONS

1. What can you say to a young painter? Go home and paint.

2. Once I was a little girl wondering how to paint moonlight on snow.

3. Sometimes it takes courage to paint a flower.

4. I can't understand people who want something and don't grab for it.

5. A house should be just a shelter. I've sometimes wished for a fire to rid me of possessions. A shell, a stone, a skull—these are enough for decoration.

6. Work is the most interesting thing one knows to do.

7. Why paint something if you don't love it?

STIEGLITZ AGING

The man explained to her—he could not stop explaining—
that a true artist like herself didn't have to travel.
I have all the world around me, he would say,
gesturing. Your thin clear air, your New Mexico highlands
would finish my heart. The handkerchief
fluttered around his mouth to ward off germs.
The woman didn't want to believe that categories
like "still vital wife" and "aging husband" belonged to them.
She had married a man of wisdom and force and genius.
Chilly days, he wore cape, herringbone coat, sweater
over shirt and tie, woolen underwear, porkpie hat
indoors. He was still a devil with the women,
at least she wondered, he photographed dear little Dorothy
nude in the meadow, vapid as a nymph by Boucher,
though thus far no guilty embrace interrupted,
no lipstick in the bathroom, no whiskers smelling of woman.
When his wife thought of the west, he knew and was afraid.
She arranged the elegant horse skull, desert-white,
and began to paint. Out there, each day arrived clear,
like the ring of a hammer striking something hard.
He liked to say to others when she was present,
there has been one who stood by me, this girl from Texas.
He spoke as if he had not learned that one who accepts disciples
invites abandonment. History was not on his side, the departing ones
told him, his holy of holies, the artist's fulfillment,
outdated and, worse, bourgeois. Her only solution
was to let the canvases of bone take shape.
She stuck a fabric flower in the empty eye socket.
The two of them held hands and listened to Beethoven.
He photographed her nude, as he had at first,

her buttocks like sacred objects, heart-shaped,
inviting the touch. From her vantage point on the mesa
the sky would be ripped by half a dozen thunderstorms at once.

They'd never wintered there. Now she was alone at the lake with only a housekeeper. She couldn't paint. Didn't want to. She couldn't bear even the thought of Alfred. New York was unthinkable.

She did have one visitor. Jean, Jean Toomer, drove up from New York to see her. She didn't mind him, he knew how to be quiet. When she opened the door and saw the look on his face, she whispered, "I've been ill, I've been ill," and fell in his arms.

They existed together quite simply. He wrote in the mornings and then read to her what he'd written. She liked the tints of his skin, caramel, café au lait, the pink undersides of his hands. He'd been a Quaker; he spoke once how the external, the color of skin, was unimportant, unreal. The inner light was what mattered. Only the incorporeal was real.

Deep snow drifted around the farmhouse. The world seemed exceedingly pure, dazzlingly bright. They drove the Model T onto the surface of the ice and walked on the wide, glowing expanse till the bitter wind forced them back. Bits of dark green, ranges of brown, and white, white. Cerulean sky. Their breath carried their words out onto the wind. When she grew cold, he took one hand in each of his and rubbed them against each other. The ice could bear so much weight, themselves and the car made no impression. The day was blown glass of finest Venetian work. She showed him her favorite birch.

In the evenings they sat by the fire. She talked, for once, about painting. Realism and abstraction were the same. The purest form of realism led to abstraction. And mere shape, a painter's envisioning of forms, pointed back toward something real. He took her hand. Both of them played with the kittens. The white kitten liked laps, her dress buttons, and his sheaf of manuscript. The firelight falling on Jean. The name "Jean" becoming a potent spell.

Oh, he must leave. She knew that, they both knew it. She had never imagined this crossroads. He would leave when she said the word. Tomorrow they would walk on the ice again.

After he left, she wrote him every day. I want you, she wrote. Sometimes terribly. But I like it that I am quite apart from you like the snow on the mountain. She did not know if she meant it.

NEW MEXICO

1

at first the hills look small

2

no rain
so the flowers didn't come

3

souvenir of the first summer
a barrel of bones

4

gray hills
all the same color and shape
a hot-colored brown hill

5

the long dark lines of the Pedernal
sky a pale greenish blue
high up, a white moon

6

the coolness and sweetness of evening
fragrance of the poison jimson weed

7

against the gray mountains
someone had imposed a cross

it was large enough to crucify a man

8

I heard the Penitente songs
and painted the dark crosses

9

the black rocks
have lain a long time
with sun and wind and blowing sand

10

keeping the fire burning
to warm where we intended to sleep

I stood on a rug and wore gloves to paint

reading *Taras Bulba* aloud
hills and stars overhead

11

gray sage, gray wet sand underfoot
gray hills, pale moon
the wind blew the coffee out of our cups

12

paintings grow by pieces
from what is around

13

low mountains covered with trees
a bare spot near the top
the shape of a leaping deer

14
painting pelvis bones
the blue from holding them against the sky

15
footmarks
around the dead cedar
he must have been dancing

GHOST RANCH

Come up to the roof! I would say.
If I can climb the ladder at my age, so can you.
Perfectly mad-looking country, isn't it,
hills and cliffs and washes thrown up by God
and left to tumble where they will.
Before the light fades, look at those gouged cliffs to the north—
a giant's sandcastle with saw-toothed turrets and spires.
Reddish rock at the bottom, then golden
solidified sand dunes, and the top's
gray fossil-filled gypsum and limestone.
See how the light hits the mountains from both front and back,
the distances appear in layers. I love to see my bare hills
glowing like red-hot coals before the abrupt dark.
With luck there'll be a thunderstorm tonight.
Our summer cloudbursts sweep in waterfalls over the rock face
and tumble down the arroyos. Sit down in that chair, I'd say,
I've brought blankets and a lantern and a pitcher of iced fruit juice.
Tell your friends in New York you spent an evening
on the roof of Ghost Ranch looking at the sky.
Rancho de los Brujos, the Spaniards called it,
which means witches, not ghosts. I've seen neither.
Come up hear around Easter, though, and you'll hear the Penitentes.
They drag their crosses and cart of death
to an unmarked chapel quite nearby.
I hear their chant, all night their one song of grief,
the high notes of a homemade flute,
the dull thuds of their cactus whips.
Their acts seem natural in a land with more sky than earth.
I never paint flowers any more.
Flowers wilt. Bone endures. Tulips often die so beautifully,

I've kept them in bowls while they withered.
A fine moon tonight, large and lopsided,
tinges of rose and almost orange.
Why would you never come here, Alfred?
The journey would not have killed you.
The clouds over Lake George are nothing to these.
In November, chamiso bushes by the road turn golden,
and the wild asters bloom. The first winter I stayed,
I remember the cows and horses grazing among the cottonwoods,
the dark mesa to the east, the jagged pink one to the west.
The very first time I came looking for Ghost Ranch,
these were the directions: follow the road northwest from Espanola,
turn where you see an animal skull.
I love the stunted piñons, the junipers and cedars.
I'd bathe in the narrow irrigation ditches.
So many different earth colors,
brown, orange, soft green, Naples yellow, even violet.
I wanted to paint with the hues of this land,
but the ocher soil was too sandy for pigment.
You aged so needlessly, Alfred. Pointlessly!
But our marriage was really very good.
You enjoyed gloom, but I could make you laugh.
I could put up with nonsense from a man
obsessed by truth. After your stroke,
when I left to come back here, you understood.
How could I paint if I stayed to hold your hand?
You told me once that true marriage is tragic;
it leads two people apart.
But we were keenly interested in each other's work.
I wish you'd been here when I did the cloud painting.

Out in the garage, nowhere else would hold it.
Hurrying to beat the cold. Then I'd climb the red hill
before sunset and look down at the cool square of sky.
Milky white. Delicate azure. A kind of glacial light.
I painted the bottom of the canvas on my knees—
what if a snake had slipped in? I have to kill them now
because of the chows. I used to scoop up the rattlers with a shovel
and pitch them outside the patio. Such elegant dogs,
their fluffy plumes, their little coyote trots.
Visitors must be careful. Their teeth are sharp.
I've seen more than one pair of shoes fill with blood.
My dear, I have a curious triumphant feeling about life.
Seeing it bleak. Knowing it so and walking into it fearless
because one has no choice. Enjoying one's consciousness.
You spoiled me for other men, you know.
How sharply the bonelight winks tonight!
Far out in the dark are hills which turn angry red
when a cloud passes. Oh, but in other lights
they are pink as flesh. What will tomorrow's first colors be?
Coral? Peach? Pale yellow? Opalescent blue?
And then the sun will rise.

NOTES

The Volcano Inside

Dedication: "For Mike, Larry, and Allen."

In the 1988 original, the first poem was "How I Wrote It." "The Reading," now the opening poem, was originally placed between "Song Without Words" and "Johnson at 34." Otherwise, the order of poems is unchanged.

"Tarklin Valley": Tarklin Valley is in East Tennessee near Cades Cove.

"How I Wrote It": The speaker of the poem is similar to, but is not, Henry Miller. One Sunday afternoon in the UTSA Library I skimmed through Henry Miller's *Tropic of Cancer*, which gave me the idea for the poem.

"Opus Posthumous": "Boerne" is pronounced "Bernie."

The Revenge by Love

Dedication: "For Allen."

The 1995 original began with an essay by Allen Hoey, "A Curious Triumphant Feeling About Life: The Poetry of David Dooley." Two poems, "Sweet Youth" and "Lillian's Elegy," have been dropped from Part I of the book. "A Little Hunger" has been moved to follow "Dirt."

Part I

"Politics": The speaker of the poem is similar to, but is not, Gore Vidal.

"And Part of Her Anus in Dallas": The title comes from the last line of an off-color limerick, as the rhythm might suggest.

"Camille in Luxor: Saint-Saens Visits Egypt, 1896": Camille Saint-Saens wrote his fifth piano concerto, the "Egyptian," in 1896 following a winter in Luxor. Saint-Saens blamed his wife, who was much younger than he, for the death of their oldest son, and broke off the marriage.

"Sun Pictures": "Sun pictures" is an early name for photographs. Eadweard Muybridge is well-known for his pioneering studies of bodies in motion. Julia Margaret Cameron is one of the most famous Victorian photographers.

Part II: *O'Keeffe and Stieglitz*

Sources for Part II include biographies of Georgia O'Keeffe by Laurie Lisle and Jan Castro; *Georgia O'Keeffe* (Viking Press, 1976), a volume of reproductions of O'Keeffe's work; and Stieglitz's photographs of O'Keeffe, reproduced in *Georgia O'Keeffe* (Metropolitan Museum of Art, no date). Some of the poems make use of O'Keeffe's own words, directly or adapted.

Alfred Stieglitz (1864-1946) was not only a pioneering photographer, but also a magazine editor and gallery owner who promoted the work of many talented artists. He immediately recognized the great ability of Georgia O'Keeffe (1887–1986). Stieglitz was separated from his wife; they had one daughter, who suffered a mental breakdown after the birth of a child ("A Conversation"). Stieglitz and O'Keeffe became lovers and married after Stieglitz and his wife divorced.

"Stieglitz Talking to the Disciples, 1916": *John Gabriel Borkman* and *When We Dead Awaken* are late plays by Henrik Ibsen.

"Lake George": The Stieglitz family had a summer home on Lake George in upstate New York.

"Judith": The bust of Judith which O'Keeffe found offensive as inferior art was in the Stieglitz family home on Lake George. Judith saved the Israelites by slaying Holofernes.

Biographical Note

David Dooley was born in Knoxville, Tennessee, and worked for many years in San Antonio. He holds a BA from Johns Hopkins University and a Master's degree from the University of Tennessee. His works include *The Volcano Inside* (1988), winner of the initial Nicholas Roerich Prize; *The Revenge by Love* (1995), which includes the sequence "O'Keeffe and Stieglitz"; and *The Zen Garden* (2004), winner of the Yellowglen Prize. He has also published numerous poems and critical articles in magazines. His work has been anthologized in *To Read Poetry*, *To Read Literature*, and *The Best Poetry of the Year*, among other collections. He has given many poetry readings and has also performed solo cabaret shows. He now lives in San Diego.